D0876441

And Live Apart

A Breakthrough Book
No. 31

And Live Apart
Poems by Molly Peacock

University of Missouri Press
Columbia & London, 1980

Copyright © 1980 by Molly Peacock
University of Missouri Press, Columbia, Missouri 65211
Library of Congress Catalog Card Number 79−3064
Printed and bound in the United States of America

Library of Congress Cataloging in Publication Data

Peacock, Molly, 1947-
   And live apart

   (A Breakthrough book; 31)
   I. Title.
PS3566.E15A8   811'.5'4   79−3064
ISBN 0−8262−0288−8

For my parents,
Pauline and Ted,
and for
my sister, Gail

Acknowledgments

These poems originally appeared, sometimes in altered versions, in the following magazines and are reprinted with their permission: "The Life of Leon Bonvin" in *Southern Review*; "Nightwake" in *Ohio Review*; "Matisse: Two Girls" in *Epoch*; "Anno Domini" and "A Kind of Parlance" are reprinted from *Shenandoah*: The Washington and Lee University Review with the permission of the editor; "Valediction" is reprinted from the *Massachusetts Review*© 1976 by The Massachusetts Review, Inc.; "Hot Spell" originally appeared as a broadside of sixty-five copies, in 1975, and is reprinted with the permission of The Bellevue Press; "Where to Play" originally appeared as a postcard, in 1978, and is reprinted with the permission of The Bellevue Press; "Two Figures" and "Two Flowers" (parts II and III from "Alibis and Lullabies") first appeared in *En Passant*; and "At the Memorial Park" is reprinted, by permission, from *Jam To-Day* #2, copyright © 1974 by *Jam To-Day*. "Peacock's Superette," "The Lawns of June," "Little Portrait," and "Safe, Safe" will appear in the *Mississippi Review*.

The generous support of the Danforth Foundation, the Mac Dowell Colony, and the New York State Arts Council CAPS Program made possible the periods of time many of these poems required.

I want to thank good friends who helped in word or spirit with this book: Milton Kessler, Joan Stein, Katie Kinsky, Katherine Kadish, Jeremy Benton, Howard C. Clark, Mary Jack, Katie Riggs, Mildred and Howard Peacock, the memory of Gilbert and Ruth Wright, and, for his endurance and advice, Thomas R. Sleigh.

M.P.
Wilmington, Delaware
9 October 1979

Contents

A Kind of Parlance, 9

Autumnal, 12

Little Portrait, 13

Good Nature, 15

Hot Spell, 18

Peacock's Superette, 19

Where to Play, 21

The Mission at Carnival, 22

Alibis and Lullabies, 25

Matisse: Two Girls, 30

Anno Domini, 33

Valediction, 34

Nightwake, 36

At the Memorial Park, 37

The Life of Leon Bonvin, 38

Reverie, 42

A Bear for the New Year, 43

In Native Tongues, 45

Walking is Almost Falling, 49

Chartreuse, 50

Children's Drawings in a Snowstorm, 52

Safe, Safe, 56

Madrigal, 58

The Lawns of June, 60

Surely if each one saw another's heart,
There would be no commerce,
No sale or bargain passe: all would disperse,
And live apart

—George Herbert

A Kind of Parlance

At 3 P.M. she feeds the penguins
in her red parka. It is a small marine zoo.

You and I are here. We hardly
know each other, this winter.

Beside her fishpail is the clipboard.
She plunges a hand in the silver mess

then pencils in who seems
to get what fish.

All the gentoo mill around her
except for Rocko, who is sick today.

These penguins do not see
very well out of water.

In the rookery they find
their partners by pitch.

This is somewhere between you
pressing against the screen yelling

Mol-llleee! and the sound of it
whispered in low registers.

But gentoo penguins see underwater
wonderfully, from their camouflage.

To the seal, the black back looks like sea.
To the fish, the white breast looks like ice.

Nor do they swim. The gentoo seem to fly. The water
is sky. The birds are water. The birds are ice.

It is very much like love,
these reversals.

The extremities of warm oils in arctic waters,
the miraculous lids of their eyes ....

The woman still called Rocko,
who stayed when the others were fed.

"Are you sick?"
She shifted the pail, straightened her back,

and dangled the last fish.
She called *rockorocko* imitating the gentoo,

a gentle, glottal sound, but somewhat loud,
again, a few times, calling from her teeth.

Rocko came slowly under her arm
at four o'clock in the winter.

She smoothed his head and asked
the questions, "What's the matter?"

"Are you sick?" "What's the matter?"
Just those questions, many times.

Near the marina ice broke against the tugs.
For a moment I felt lifeless,

like the time when I was kept,
for some symptom of my eyes, in a dark room.

I wanted to smoke, or to drink,
or to leave very quickly—then saw

the shoulders of your jacket against the sky
and made the gesture which became a necessity, to look
    up —

and there was no place to go which was right.
So I faced

the fact of our proximity
and the desire I knew

we both felt, to move
slowly under the arm of that woman.

By the rookery, battened for the night,
we both began speaking gentoo.

I whispered *rockorocko* in a low register,
and you asked, in the voice of the woman,

"Are you sick?" so I said, "What's the matter?"
and we echoed the questions gently back and forth,

the two questions, in the midst
of *rockorockos*.

Autumnal

It is tiring to the arms, this weather.
Late produce lines the roadside stands, red
by gray by red by gray, the frame the same as the picture.

Keep on going. Clouds bunch the horizon like
    schoolchildren
on the stairways home. Home and free, here,
wrap up in this, a cottage blanket, thanks.

Fine? Yes, I . . . Yes, I . . . Fine? Fine.
The afternoon light waves gracefully, Bye,
like a dancer turned teacher somewhere

achieves a radiance in demonstration,
and her young student waves in sudden
radiance, after.

A scarf of birds lights on our two trees, nicknamed
Death and Dying. We've been waiting for the geese.
This was good, but wait until the geese.

There is a fire in my soul. It does not belong in this poem.
Like love, how seldom it belongs in the human room:
That chair. That energetically braided rug. That
    awkward pair of shoes.

Little Portrait

from Vermeer's *A Lady Writing*

The room is dark, but my robe shines
as if a small sun had risen.
It is the light he paints me in.

At my desk, my desk among the things
askew I know so well, the quill,
the vellum, my necklace worn

for a moment in the glass
and removed, I review the post
and respond. This time I do it quickly,

clean from my bath, my hair tied,
freshly jacketed, intent to speak back
to those who have spoken to me.

My work is quiet and rapid
in the dark room. I have decided things,
things which lay on my mind.

The letters are a way of knowing,
and knowing is remembering
which appointments I choose to keep

and which to put off. What
makes me look up? A sharp
movement he makes. He

is painting me, at my desk.
Now, the expression on my face
is hard for me to know here behind my teeth

and skull. What do my muscles, nerves,
and sinews show? I trust
I will recognize my face

for I have seen it now all my life
in its quandaries caught here and there
in mirrors above the goods

on scales, and all of the times
where I had time to look. In looking
there is an element of coercion,

something must be forced beyond vanity.
After a glance at the pearls
caught at the throat, then the face—

its dignity, its deep personal arousal
and startled gladness—an affirmation
that what is in the mind, in the face

is true, is truer, as the body
is a bit truer in the making of love
than in the making of the usual living lies.

Good Nature

People often hate the flowers
grown by their aunts and mothers.
They say it is tradition
not to like geraniums
or chrysanthemums, whatever

is planted in continuum.
Outside the red house
lies a bed of petunias,
sticky, like annually
half-licked candy.

It keeps the bugs away.
Takes no care but
weekend watering.
Petunias grow all by themselves!
By Memorial Day—

the day I always fail
to make it home before—
they stick resolutely
in the righted ground.
There is nothing you can do.

Oh who cares what is planted there.
Though when I came this year,
the bed lay as undisturbed
as a mattress in an old garage:
a sudden, windy entourage

of snapdragons and bachelor's buttons,
a girl's haphazard garden
drawn on manila paper,
loomed in my mind for a moment
as if it were stapled

to a public school bulletin board.
Then the vision was erased.
In a cunning integration
of the Bible and evolution
our science teacher, Mr. Reuss,

introduced our class to insects.
They, he told us, were the meek
who would inherit the earth.
"Yuck! Mr. Reuss!" I was
appalled and continued to seek

a way to return human to meek.
Earlier gardeners of this patch
found their way in a lolling,
slightly medicinal cache
of petunias nestled by the porch.

Anger descends on me—descended
on me then—as confusion.
Weren't the meek the delicate?
The delicate, me? No, n-no.
Now, the strict reality

is the need for what won't expire
in the sun and the desire
not to see the meek
reminders of what's after
the human peak hanging

resolutely from each leaf,
bud, and at dusk, boring
through the window screens.
I bought fourteen flats
of young petunias and a mean-

edged trowel and dug
eighty-four holes. Petunias
smell like Vicks Vapo Rub.
But they *like* the things,
like Mr. Reuss liked

the thousand legs and wings
crawling over the shards of man.
I saw, for a moment,
a vision of my garden again.
I hate being wise.

I hate the garden of compromise
made from a need
to surrender human need
to oblige necessity.
Reverence for death,

to them, means growth.
And I hate the years of knowing,
logical, biological,
hereditary—and heretical—
they insist is flowering.

Hot Spell

Water dies overnight
on the nightstand.
Listen, below a needle
dives in and out of cotton.
Children float down the driveway
to a thin racket in the street—
"You'll strangle the poor things!"

Long distance
your mother tells you
something you never knew.
Your knees crack
like crabshells.
Out front the substitute mailman
stumbles on the high step.

Fillets slap the ice.
It is fish day at the grocery,
where the shelves bloat
with spiral notebooks.
In three more weeks: School.
Soon you will not hear your first name
spoken in daylight.

Peacock's Superette

There were plenty of cans
to wipe off every week
in Peacock's Superette. The fans
at the back of the store hummed
like dusty electrical bees,
blowing the old exhaust
into a graveled parking lot.
Peacock's sold beer—most
brands—local ale, pop, and fought
the supermarkets down The Boulevard
for cigarettes. It sold Tom
Collins mix and Bloody
Mary juice, peanuts, chocolate Pom
Poms, anything at all for company
some member of a family
was volunteered to run out and get.
It specialized in what
people in busy big shops forgot
and hadn't the heart to go back for.
It was a neighborhood store,

on The Boulevard, full of chain
groceries, developments, and traffic
to Niagara Falls. Six profane,
black jacketed, laughing
boys gasolined the parking
lot, and Ma went out with a lit
cigarette and said she'd spark
the fire and be happy to be rid of it.
So they cleared off.

                Peacock's
had the mind of an invalid: gumption
and a will to self-destruction. The locks
were re-secured, just as if it mattered.

At 2 the string beans from grade school,
then at 2:30 the little shrimps
from junior high descended; the coolers
were raided; at 4 the shadowed, limp
women for one or two things
they'd forgotten; and at 5
the hoarse riveters or truck
drivers or steel men joked
or were glum at the counter. Luck
was what each of them talked.
The sickly lamps swung
upside down from their stalks
like mechanical herbs hung
up to dry, the dust on the cans
the old pollen. Men with the red
eye of drink often took in their hands
their old gray handkerchiefs, said
"Hello," and sneezed.
The traffic went by
our awful green sign—

"Nice night." *"It's slow."* "Life's
no good for the working man.
Them damn Canucks knife
the good jobs and work for shit,"
says one. *"I know."* "My TV broke,"
an old man says, "I left
my keys ahome. I'm locked
out good."

   —hung like the last leaf
on God's barren branch,
turning above the deaf,
the deafening traffic to the Falls, lynched
and left for show, like memory or old
forgotten knowledge become belief
on its crooked pole.

Where to Play

Near here is a Catholic family.
They have a retarded boy.
Please play with him nicely
and don't give him any toys.

They've fenced off the corner with poplars.
They've junked up the yard with machines.
Don't peer through their branches,
they'll come for you.

The door to the room is great-grandma's.
There's lace in there.
Play in the front by the rocker,
it's safer.

Pound Chopin on the black keys.
Pound Mozart on the whites.
Don't wake grandma, she's sleeping.
She's dead in there, dead in there,
with lace all spilt from her mouth.

The Mission at Carnival

A Dream

On carnival night
each winking light on the strings
crisscrossing the ordinary plain
(all dusted for carnival night)
seems to be moving.

Broad light stays still.
The flood of light from out the flaps
of the booths and tents beyond the mission
makes places for the faces in shadow
to emerge, blink, and enter,

enter and disappear.
Feeling lost is part of walking through
carnivals at night, for none of the places
we wander in and out of is built to stay.
Decked out in stripes

above windows and doors,
tenting yawns from the mission walls
in festive disguise of the old building's
permanence. It is utterly open in the dark,
light streaming

from those billowing
apertures. It is dusty stone and stucco,
like what Jesus might have stumbled into.
I am hungry enough to forsake company,
penny throwing, shooting

ranges, and feathered prizes
and to act in the desperation the lonely show
(what makes any possible friend avoid us)
if that will find me food. In this dream —
and I am in a dream,

            searching for the exact
right place to eat, as if I were shopping
for the thin lost clothes I wore in a dream
while quite awake in a real bazaar, and of course
            not finding them—

            the mission is empty.
The walls glow as if by candlelight,
but more ancient, as if by torchlight.
Here, there are the right tables and chairs.
            I choose a small

            empty table, all
dressed in white cloth, wonder if I am to pay
and wonder if I should be here, suddenly
not believing in anything, thinking perhaps
            this is not a place

            to eat, after all.
But it is so plain and quiet and warmly lit
I hope to stay. White bowls of varying
sizes and a large white plate at my place:
            one little bowl

            is surely for coins
and one for the head of a flower.
It is quiet, the quiet where we hear
low small noises we ordinarily fail to hear.
            A monk of strict

            order appears.
I know no manners to draw on,
and much is almost spoken through
my nervousness. By what signal will
            I place my order?

            The bowl for coins
is turned away, and to my place the brother
brings a favorite meal. Not a favorite meal
of now, but what I liked to eat long ago,
            meat afloat in brown

gravy on the plate,
green peas perched in a separate bowl.
Do I speak now? I look, and the monk
in all exasperation breaks a vow,
"It is to eat!"

It is for me,
and I have the meal, eating slow,
as if my mouth is small and it is long ago.
Outside the deep window people walk
beneath the lights

all blinking yes,
and off, saying leave, saying stay,
as the people are leaving, as the people
decide to stay, turning all around
to leave and stay.

But the strings of lights
are probably quite still. And the pulse of off
and on probably regular. Yet how they seem
to move more toward and recede farther away.
They are the lights

of carnival night.
Their uncertainty and the awkward pattern
of lanterns make life feel lost. Out there
is not the dust earlier walked, but beaten,
unsure and empty.

Alibis and Lullabies

I

Weeds among wire in the snow
under duress of freezing rain.
How remarkable a face they will show
frozen in the slow sunrise tomorrow.

But it is today in the red house.
Listen to what I say:
what was is dying
and gives a choice of misery.

The past steered away
in its long black coat
all mussed with ashes
from the ladies' cigars it smoked.

I have two dreams of flying.
One follows the river,
the other one flies into wires.
That is the one with lucky bad luck,

a trinket from Fate, like a look
at the ice tiara before
I drive the road tomorrow.
So I wonder what small good news,

a lost letter, a job offer,
will arrive on the day of Past's death,
among the cinders of this house
and the crystals of Its breath.

II

What is bright or rare here is called oriental.
This is the West, and it is home.
We are afraid of something here: the ornamental.
You know the pictures where the blue foam

rises in vicious coils and stops above
those two small figures, but it looks so calm?
Where home is, is plain, water only water, and the love
those two must feel for one another under the bomb

and blast of their ocean is unspeaking—as the tiny
china figures in a closet in this house will not come alive
but are alive, even though they are cold to the tiny
hands who wish them, will them, breathe them alive,

and almost see each mouth open in each head,
and if they be broken, be sure they are dead.

III

Two irises in a glass. It is not that it is *all* wrong.
They intertwine like the arms and legs of stuffed
animals on their bench in someone's old white room,
or leaning dancing dolls. I wish I knew

what is plain to everyone else. Something must be
plain to them, they are all carrying on their lives,
according to me. Beyond the iris, beyond the iron
railing, wrens drop from the tree to the ground.

They don't bother to flutter, they just
move a bit into the air and drop
like a girl or boy who takes steps

three at a time. Yes, I am sad here in the dust.
I wish I knew what was plain to everyone else,
according to me, and according to me.

IV

It is not the case that a light shuts off
or a part of the mind, or the world, goes dark.
Everything gradually blurs, the shock
is only when a sudden memory clears.

What was and a vision of what is
walk down a long pew and meet
on a day when nothing broken can be fixed,
and everything is noticeably much more worn.

Layer after layer of gauze has fallen over
or layer on layer of color weathered off—
if only the mind were a barn,
if only a body waiting to be dressed.

V

I got a two-wheeler for my birthday,
a compliment from grandfather,
and rode a big bike early,
at four impatient years of age.

Since I was a little girl,
he put the training wheels on, and off
I went, down the three houses worth
of walk that was my road, on past

a dozen houses-to-be of field.
In four or so more years the block was full,
and I still rode with the training wheels.
Sarcastic new neighbors asked *what*

I was in training *for*.
I was in training not to fall.
The world was spinning seventeen miles per hour,
as it does still.

VI

I left him at the table examining old coins.
One he had spied from the tractor,
where he had tilled for years looking down
and once before found a spoon.

There were many speculative nights,
times when we'd read a fat
historical novel or seen a movie set
in the Middle Ages, when he or I

asked what we would have been then,
in those days. There was always
a princess in soiled clothes who was noble.
Long ago it was me, but I wouldn't say so.

In later years we chose the century
we'd rather live in. "But I'd be dead," I'd say,
"of an awful disease, or maybe dead at birth."
If I wouldn't be noble, I'd rather be gone

than to spy the truthful answer
standing (I wasn't that frail
and wouldn't have failed so easy)
in the hut off the field, at the hole

for a door, the one with lank hair
and grimy, muscular feet,
not crazy enough to be locked up,
sullen and tolerant like everyone else.

VII

This is to explain my cruelty.
This is to explain the cruelty of my thirtieth year.
Now I spend all daylight hours awake, and the fear,
a fear of the world in its globe tangibly,

I can explain it no better than the outside fiercely
active and not a part of me, is now a near
steady pulse I hear then don't hear but don't care
to forget, since it is me and I have changed and the
    cruelty

comes from fearing to forget an original self.
To want a part of the self is to push those who are else
away. So they become part of the world,

and I am of and afraid of the world,
as if I were in great need of food, that kind of savagery,
or for my life, guarding a prisoner, that kind of savagery.

VIII

And this is how
the stars come out.
The first says Yes, the second Hello,
the third one says Good-morrow.

Yes, hell-, yes, -o, yes, good-
morrow. The fourth says Welcome-to-you.
Home-at-last-my-dear, the fifth one says.
The tenth will take your coat-and-hat

and hang-them-up-for-the-morning.
The twenty-fifth star gives the twenty-fifth welcome,
strung like an alphabet, minus one.
How-do-you-do-happy-to-see-you

and all else lost in the chorusing
yes, hello, good morrow!
The stars are out. Yes, it *is* a windy night.
They blow their greetings down like ...

... like a scarf almost lost on a corner
wraps suddenly back on your collar.
A felt moment of astonishment: Fate sees a need is met.
Each point of the night like the lights of a city bus

far away down the street coming toward you.
It will take you home through the cold night air,
and if the stars had hands, they might comb your tangled
    hair,
if the stars had hands, they might warm you.

Matisse: Two Girls

I know who they are. That one's me,
the brunette on the right. The blond
in the yellow dress is you.

It's a picture without protection
like the snaps of us on our vacations
with the sun in our eyes. But here we are inside

a perfect summer house, like mine
when I was married and rich, with cool walls
and enormous windows flung open behind us

to the tops of old maples. They are not maples
in the *picture* — they are green clouds slashed
with brown stripes — but don't you like to look

at the places and faces in pictures to find out
where and which you are? I must be
the frightened one in blue, after my affair

with your husband. By the indictment of
your pointed nose, chin, elbows thrust
from that yellow dress, I know. Is yellow

the fiercer color? Or blue.
Well, the figure I chose as you —
her hair's too short, for one thing.

I thought it was you, since neither girl
will look at the other, but it is not us.
There is no wine, no cigarettes,

and the flowers on the table are too fresh.
I just cut them from my mother's garden,
having gotten up and dressed and almost

beaten my mother to the breakfast table.
But evidently she had eaten long before,
since there, in the picture,

the table's set only for one. The late one.
She has already watched the sunrise and has turned
away from the window to stare at the floor.

But her body sits toward me,
my arms stuck under my breasts, anticipating
the explosion—for having slept, for having cut . . .

for having what? A blue dress?
I wait for the hair to toss or
the figure to turn. It does not.

In fact, my mother turns to me quite often.
The blowsy head in the picture can't be her.
Look how young the girl in blue is,

how carefully she holds herself.
Her hair is parted so nicely,
as though she cared for it.

It is the color of the antlered branches
behind her, and her dress matches the sky.
What a burden she has to distinguish herself!

She must be a younger sister. Mine.
So the woman in yellow is me,
the pointed nose, the pointed chin,

the angularity in the summer room.
And my frightened younger sister,
newly married in this lovely summer house,

with such first luck at flowers
that she cannot be sure it is her talent,
has cut these roses to placate me,

because she cannot see my face
and watches only the points
seeming to pivot toward her.

But I am standing here,
and I do not mistake
where the rude lines originate.

Anno Domini

It is Palm Sunday, when Jesus rides into Jerusalem,
the brightest picture in the Bible book.

Despite the two dimensions, air
is moving, molecular with spring,

is sweeter, even in this old apartment,
a quintet with Savior and winds.

How porous houses are, to let it in!
If I were directing a comic film of my life,

I'd open with Jesus in Jerusalem,
my mother on the stucco balcony, breaking

off a palm and giving it to me
with instructions to run and wave it

at Jesus. I would take a step and jerk the palm
sideways, and look at her, then up and back,

and look at her, step by step all the way down
until the procession had almost passed,

asking with each spasm of the palm,
Is this right? No, is this right?

Valediction

We live without children,
give presents
to nieces,
think why not
and then do not—
there is something in solitude,
there is.

Hard to see
the hawkweed picked.
Want to say,
"You won't have them for,"
then recall she
has no children.
Next year
doesn't matter.

You know he drowned
saving his little girl
in the Delaware.
We write his wife
but whisper,
"It's not good,"

for the other one
who lay on the bed.
Whose tiny hairs around her breasts
he counted
as his little girl counted
her foreign money,
rupees, dinarae.
The thousand freckles on her back
only the sack of lira could match.

There is something in
the construction of flesh.

What else in life?
Istanbul, maybe, a man
whose nipples harden
faster than one's own.

Among seaweed and algae,
by the inner tube so hot
the flies won't touch it,
his head, his arm,
the eye that counted.

What will the little girl
say when she grows up?
But it does not concern
growing up.
It concerns life jackets,
swimming lessons at thirty-five
when childless she decides,
when because of her children
she thinks why not
and then does not —
if there is something in solitude,
it is a head face
down, an arm, an eye
that counted.

Nightwake

To startle in the garden and think of you dead,
to veer and find my victim not victimized again,
to fall asleep mouth open and wake
alarmed and muggy soon again —

it is June, that month of fathers and daughters,
when roses are a constant dozen in my married room.
Just what could my father have done then,
that I would want advice from the twelve of you?

I willed him dead at the age of six
and said hello to corpses ever since.

Now to wake from thick dreams of flowers
cut with a family blood,
shift fast in the bed and stiffen,
listen to his breathing to make sure,
want him waking and saying any good thing he knows —

let him sleep.
Face the shut beauties on the bedroom table.
Who needs a dozen silent friends?
It is dangerous to say your good things to them.
It is sentimental to say them to yourself.

Where do you go to say them
when this narrow night refuses them?

Out on Brown Road the body is flat as the black meadow.
If someone came to the side of you now,
they would walk off the edge of the earth.

At the Memorial Park

His dark head lifts, like a stringed instrument,
and commences.
His voice is perfect.
I think it must open granite.

Two women are climbing toward us
with geraniums.
There is something I want before they reach us.

It is March, but today it snowed.
I expected to see a few willows in bloom.
Across the path I thought there was a cottontail,
but it was paper trembling.

The Life of Leon Bonvin

Leon Bonvin was a painter,
a watercolorist, in France
in the last century. He lived
in the country, a second son.
His father kept the inn, BONVIN.

Elder brother lived in Paris,
where he fed, sketched, bought oils, canvas,
and sundry extraordinary
horsehair brushes and quills. Bonvin
stayed home, although he was allowed

a short study in the city.
Goodwine: fine wines. There is nothing
against a man who wants a good name
kept above his tavern doors
and keeps his son at home

drawing water, asking the girls
politely to clear the tables,
watching the growing pile of stained
linens. At dusk or at dawn when
the suspenders of his father

dangle from a brass hook inside
the bedroom door, the painter paints.
There will be hours of men against
the tavern walls, and an hour
of sleep for Bonvin, drying hours

for the tints. Only at dawn and
only at dusk, in the barest
sufficiency of natural light
and in the barest absence of
père's powdery wheezes, "Son! Son!"

and when the brunette tendrils of
his young wife's hair are curled in sweat
above the bread oven—early,
when the inn is empty, or late,
when maids agree to serve alone

the ox-driving customers till
supper—Bonvin, a man of good
name, but always in haste, gathers
his paints to confront the light death
of sunset, or the death of dawn.

Extraordinary roses, dried
in layers of black beneath red,
the green vase, green as in bottles
of Beaujolais, the uneasy
gray light beneath fog ascending

out the open windows. There are
no figures in this work. Still life.
The continuing absence of sun.
In the blackened landscapes of dusk,
the bits of rouged spots, are they blooms?

It is difficult to see, it
is impossible to see—what
is that in the undergrowth, there:
Couldn't he have imagined light?
But they are beautiful. The fury

they breed. Did they bring him to speech
in the ill-lit tavern by day,
by morning his vista in fog,
by evening almost in final,
almost in ludicrous darkness?

Leon Bonvin, with two pails on
his shoulders, followed by his small
rambunctious sons upstairs to all
the rooms lined every other one
like headstones. "These times of day

are minor times!" The heart wants
midnight, or it wants noon . . . .
                                        After
1864 and '65,
the most frantic years, the years
in which flowers looked like crepe, skies

like the linen of the moon's hood,
where the number of paintings done
times the number of wheezing calls
of père Bonvin, blurred by welcomes,
thank-yous, and francs on the tables,

caused the damnation of his lids
drooping by a line from his brows,
caused the growth of an astounding
unlaundered pile of aprons fouled
with rosé, red wine, white, sweat, and

clogged brushes, Bonvin painted less
and less, then took his own life.
The artists of his time, who were
unknown to the artist alive,
auctioned his finished work abroad

on behalf of elder brother,
for the maintenance of the inn—

the sign of the tavern BONVIN
hung in the morning in fog—for
the burial of fils Bonvin,

for the food, rooms,
and well-being
of his widow,
and the schooling
of her two sons.

Reverie

It comes in the morning through all the rooms,
when the mind stays a long time with sleep
as in a meditation, or when toast,

or sunlight, or the lateness of the hour
do not matter. The one with whom I share
my life is away. *Take care, it's raining,*

a'tu une parapluie? It is a density.
The head might fill with rage or might
drain into the little blue glass which looks

as though it holds that litter of chartreuse trees
just behind it, out the window, beyond the cabin.
Take care, take care of the crowds,

a-tu ton compas d'esprit? It is a necessity.
There is a time in the morning when the padding
through rooms ends, when the hands are folded
    in a chair

as in a meditation, *love me, remember me*,
above the black hair. The little sugar bowl,
the rose glass in the light with the knob

in the shape of a star:
eight points, every earthly direction—
North, Northease, East, Southeach,

South, Southwish, West, Northwhere.
In the noise and the swell and the ease and the wail,
a red speck of feet under wings, *take care.*

A Bear for the New Year

The January bear is bright.
He belongs to you.
All the white
snow beyond is blue, blue.

Now hang the calendar
low—let's see the number.
Day 1 of the new year
we'll spend in awkward slumber.

The bear has his mouth open wide.
What has he said?
Now look inside
so his secrets can be read.

The bear is old. He is a fitting
age for the new year.
All your unwitting
youth, in his presence, is clear.

January's light taunts
old bear on his way,
but he knows the best haunts,
where to wait and what to say.

You don't know what to expect
and assume you may
push the bad breaks away.
Whatever happens is perfect,

I say, say, 31 times.
You think you will witness 31 crimes.
In fact they will only be 31 rhymes
with whatever our destinies will for our primes.

Each day is perfect for me and you.
It's heartlessly ambiguous:
we call the snow's genus
white when in fact it's blue;

we call ourselves "us"
when we are me and you.
In life the odd is always true;
raucous, then fabulous,

numerous, then few.

In Native Tongues

Mother there is water in the air
Yes and there is air in water
Mother the baby has no voice
Speak baby
Mother the baby will not speak
My mirror is broken
Yes it is, yes it is, I found a sliver!

       *

Mother people here have trouble with their fires
but I do not
You have a knack
No I do not care if I am cold

       *

Mother the longer I live the lower my voice goes
I know
It is deeper
and full of the sex in it
I know
Mother there is a hidden spring here
They say bring water for your animals
they will live longer
I know
But you have never been here
I know
My animals will have deep voices
Not as deep as if I were their mother

       *

Mother I read a story
and it plagued me

I see you found another sliver
Mother I gave the story back
But you remember

          *

Mother you have never grieved in your life
That is true
Mother I will go away
I have never grieved in my life

          *

Mother Mother Mother!
You sound like a baby
I know
The baby in me waited a long time
So, that is not over

          *

Mother I have a pet, a little bird
Eat it
I am human
But you growl

          *

Mother sometimes I am alone and sometimes
    with someone
Good, it is good to eat alone and sleep in a pack
It is not a pack, it is one or two humans
I am natural
I am natural

          *

Mother I do not come from you
You come also from your father

Where is he
By the fire
That is the fire I made with one match
Yes his hands are cold

He is at the fire but I have never asked him
Yes it is too bad
He might have given or he might not
Father says I look cold

Tell him he is wrong

        *

Here take my medals Mother
My hands are full

Hold them in your mouth
My mouth is for meat

A mouth can hold many things
Yes I know what you hold in your mouth

And what is that
A human cock

Yes I swallow fire
But you are lonely

        *

I bring my blanket Mother
but the sun goes in
Wrap in your blanket

I lie on my back Mother
and wait for my lover
That sun will go in too

If it does I will do for myself
What do you think the sun does behind its cloud?

*

Mother if you stand in the sun you cast
no shadow and if I sit beneath you
I receive no protection

I am not the shade

Walking is Almost Falling

In saying no, you felt as though you lied,
wrecking an old self. But did you wreck it?
Then, from under, the world began to slide.

In fact, you told the truth when you replied.
You took the step and finally saw it fit,
but saying no, you felt as though you lied.

The great snows gone, the galactic glide
begun, the mud-pink gums of earth were lit
by sun, and then the world began to slide.

Its tongue roiled up and curved. You tried
to walk at first—and could, a little bit!
—but stepping so, you felt as though you lied,

for the warm world felt false. It did not hide
its self. Walking on the crust employed your wit:
Said yes. Then stepped. (This way the world won't slide.)

But walking on open earth is choice; the tide
of all acceptance is unloosed. Truth, it
is unsteady, the old glum world begins to slide.
You hurt so, saying no, and feel as though you lied.

Chartreuse

The green parakeet walls of our kitchen
hurt my eyes, but I loved the name of that
color, chartreuse. I was ill and, like that word,
warm, small, delicate and foreign myself.

—How long was I supposed to lie in the dark?
I heard things through a kind of smoke, as if
I were a genie at the bottom of a jar
who uncurled slightly shocked when the lid

was uncapped, and a word or two swirled down
through my master's cigar.   —"What's that color?"
Sickness nearly destroys time. The French word
lay in my mother's mouth. "Chartreuse. Feeling

better?" I'd come downstairs for a first try.
"Like this new color?" It was like the wings
of our parakeets, our ... budgerigars.
"Chanteuse?" I said. "It sounds like a song,

doesn't it? No, char-treuse." Parakeets
split seeds in their beaks, then spit the pulp at
whomever they're fond of, their children,
their mates, themselves in their mirrors, or

very often at mother or me. Crack
chew, spit, squawk, and sing. They spat in a
beautiful wet trajectory right from
their blue tongues to my little coated one.

It's a nice feeling, but shocking, the pulp
doesn't quite belong there, but you'd never want
to spit it out. I liked the way my mother
cracked chartreuse. I took it quick as a lozenge.

Then my eyes blurred and burned, so I
stepped backward, tripping over the kitchen stool,
landing in the doorway to the living room,
where no lights were on. It was a rainy day.

I lay on the dampish gray wool rug
like a rug on the bottom of a bottle
staring up at the wavering chartreuse light
blurring, then clearing, like a face in love

brought so close it blurs, then is held away
to flower, a bright nugget flowering,
growing the way things grow, opening
from all its sides, hectic, then royal and slow.

"Chartreuse," I said. Time to be back in bed.

Children's Drawings in a Snowstorm

A Knight, a Squire, a Deep-sea Diver, a Doctor, a Dancer,
and Thanksgiving Turkeys

The story in heaven says a mad old woman
plucking goose after goose and hurling down the
    pinions

is the maker of our snowstorms. The geese,
they are the wind in the net of her frustration.

She died and was sent to heaven
and having to stay there makes her mad,

for she hates being dead twice,
forever dead in heaven and deadened all her life—

having always done the opposite of what she meant.
The afterlife didn't change that.

When the world is frozen, she screams, "Move!"
But down here, taped up in the kitchen,

a lady, five gentlemen—and two turkeys—
claim smaller rights of expression.

On the refrigerator door, a cutout man
with a doctor's bag and an oversize hat

walks beside a cutout dancing girl.
The Knight of the Silver Shield and Sir Yellalot

sit by a deep-sea diver on the freezer top.
Below them perch two Thanksgiving turkeys.

"Uh oh," says the knight, "I've lost my shield.
No battle today!" "Have you seen my treasure ?"

says the diver, "well, that's ok,
I search much faster when nothing's at stake."

"But I've taken an oath, quite sincerely. I'm NOT a fake.
I'll fix anyone who wants me, but to tell you the truth,
   dear,

I've battened my hat down over my ears," says the
   doctor,
"can't hear tucked away in here." "Madame!

it is my doom," pouts the dancer,
"to dance only in my room!"

And the turkeys in their tropical getups cry,
"We'll be eaten for dinner, yi, yi, yi, yi!"

The little pictures do and do and do.
They are so anxious to please.

Look what we have made!
Drawn and bordered, empty, detailed, and staid.

We want to be best in our class, they cry,
and trotted home and pasted up!

I suddenly think of all I'd trade for love
and love's satiation, all the attention

these pictures get paid . . . .
You dumb little dancer, go find yourself a partner,

you yell, you fight, you run, you find that treasure!
It's time, scaredy-doctor, to start hearing people die.

That is what we live for,
what the mad old woman is sore for—

oh kids, don't think she's grandma in heaven
plucking a goose for the pot

to make God His Sunday dinner.
She's twice a loser and that's why she makes winter.

No teacher will look at a simple, measly truth:
and so one hides his shield, another shuts his mouth.

I was scared—am scared—there wasn't
a prize of praise to be won for my heart, either.

What made you all? The same as made me,
I guess, the same as made the pumpkin-shaped

world all round, the same mistaken and loving
hands who taped you up and said, "Well done."

This little gallery cannot talk,
though I'm awfully scared somehow

that they will move in their group and turn
like the murky videotapes they show as proof of ghosts,

then quietly and forever face the wall.
Oh don't!

What is delicate in life, what is tousled
and green and small might at any minute go . . .

to dance alone, to fail to doctor,
look my little gobblers,

you've *got* to run away
if you know you'll be eaten for dinner,

my diver, you've got to find your treasure
. . . and with it love, so seriously green and small.

That was me who said "oh don't" to them
in the voice I might use, dear God who am I, with a lover.

There will be school today. The plows are out.
She lies exhausted in Paradise.

She makes me want to be alive in life.
Outside the fields were built up by the storm.

They stand and nearly shiver,
hairless, treeless, and reborn.

I hear the voices people use,
sometimes, in TV interviews

after disaster has flooded their home
or taken it by fire, or they've stood

at the mouth of a fallen mine
speaking in shock, the words of humankind.

It is the pictures,
talking as we talk when our faces

are buried in the arms or bellies
of our friends.

I feel as though I've fallen asleep in the party
and woken up on the couch very late at night.

My sister, my mother, my oldest friends
are at the table, talking and cleaning up.

Their voices are tired and low,
they brush each other's arms . . .

but it is the morning, before school,
and the snow has stopped,

and it is the pictures who talk,
"Love seemed enormous

and the width of our embrace seemed small.
Desire and loneliness made us."

Safe, Safe

for Corrine, Marc, Nancy, and Phil

Now the small shepherds of the timothy
rove the fields again, the monarchs and light
tame yellow fieldflies and new ones no one
knows the name of, wet dark little mutants
batting two tangerine eyes from each wing.

In another dining room, long, cool, as full
of summer as the queens and bears and dippers
in the summer night sky can fill it, rose-
green curtains open and billow to show
and close the night, and a man rises
to pour his four friends drinks when all of them
are as tired as he. The exhausted accents
of all our home towns on our tongues, vowels
of sleepiness, and happiness, make us poke
fun at one another at the expense
of the accentless speech of the world each
of us had to, or only did, in five parts
of the world, acquire. The long spires of the drinks,
the listening and murmuring and slapping
of cards, and the lips on the spires of the drinks;
it is summer. We are tired.

                         The butterflies
have returned to the fields because of the lack
of insecticides. A few must have been there
all along increasing in number, but
it seemed as though they disappeared, then came
back in a hoard, infinite, fluttering, tame,
calm, like memories. So often our childhood
worlds are huge and glittering, or frightening,

that finally when we recall a scene,
like a manila drift of wings in timothy,
what happened seems like fantasy.
The fieldflies were not missed when they were gone,
as we learned not to miss the things we could
not have. When those desires became the past, they
felt silly to remember, vaporous
and dangerous. But the hundreds of wild
monarchs I see, I see now I *saw*—they *were*
facts. They are real. It is safe. It is science!

Nothing to do with false remembering.
The world and its migrations continue past
wondering. We are real. What on earth
must have happened to me that a loss
of that loss would bring tears to my eyes.
How little I allow myself to miss,
or feel. The rinds of limes lie watery in each
glass, we make each touch goodnight, goodnight,
how increasingly we have kissed each other.
And leaned and mocked and rubbed and grinned and
    borrowed
from each other. Look at our tired shoulders.

Goodnight, goodnight, we take the oily cards
and damp used glasses with us. And you to bed, too . . . .
Tell me you adore me. I adore you!
The lights go off in other rooms and curtains move.
Nazdrowie! Yes, yes. And for you. Yes, darling.

Words. The old words.

Madrigal

If you are to walk down this sidewalk made
slender by the open stalls of fruit, pears,
prickly pears, plums, past the stalls of onions and
the carrots lined side by side in a wooden
tray like enlisted men lined up asleep
in a slatted bed in an old fort, then
you will find the street. Your progress is slow,
but you are not jostled or pushed in the crowd
because it is early, so everything
is slow, and you are among the old women
who dream through the market in all
the tongues of their girlhoods every morning.
It is just cooling off, it is fall.
At this corner you turn and walk uphill.
If you were a self-respecting indoor
plant, a vine perhaps, who had grown by an open
window or on a porch or iron stairway
all summer and were now taken in,
you would see on your long lead runner the nodes
of white possible roots if someone were to
pin you down against the soil at the rim
of the pot. Somehow this will not be so,
but were it so, you would be ready. This was
a season *magnifico*. You are healthy
and sleepy. Wake up, *fanciulla*, take the stairs.
In this tall city life on the third story
takes place in its heart, the place to which you
or anyone like you is embraced and
kept close to the chest of this place for it
is no longer so hot that the sweat of both
your bodies would make sleeping alone
the ultimate comfort. In fact you have

58

come here to go back to sleep. Open the door.
You are not so young a woman that
you need to worry if you will remember
what happens for the rest of your life
as you did when you held moments in doorways,
in halls, or cloakrooms so fast they fled. There
he is in the bed with the newspapers
you are crushing now. You are, neither of you,
pretty, or still. Your photographs, both of you,
have always been caught in moments too small for you.
Now you move and talk, laugh, groan, cough, and kiss.
Something in a glass is caught before it spills,
and the bag of irresistible pears rolls
across the floor; sheets, sun, shucked off clothes: time,
the movement in intimate bondage of notes
that say we are what is, life like bobbins
of pale and bright thread blowing across
the earth, the blowing of light across the bed,
eyes cognac, then umber, that nose, your
glasses and knees, a kind of music, isn't it?
reposing and unraveling, separate,
unloosing, as the voices in the market,
as the loose, close clouds in a sky of fall
light high above this city where weather
shows only in the spaces between its stories,
as if the city were a forest, light
coming only through the canopy of branches
who lean, muse, and weave what we are
to mean and be.

The Lawns of June

The lawns of June, flush with the walks and white
driveways of town, grow and are mown. The grid
of lawn after lawn, then drive after drive,
the 90-degree angles of walks, roads
stripped and then tarred flush with the curbs, all these,
smooth, regular as the rules on a fresh
white card pulled from the box of a new game,
or fresh and regular as the game board
itself, the squares prime for our leaping plays,
are what any troubled mind or body
would order: such as, from here to the drug
store is forty-seven lawns, one hundred-
six lawns from here to the veterinary.
It feels good to count in these ways. And smooth,
the sidewalks and streets are very smooth.
An octagonal sign says Stop. Two lines
mean School. The lawns are thick chartreuse gouache,
roads black as silk, straight and fine as surgical
silk, the walks are bandage white. How smooth and
fast the wheels of cars and bikes and skates go,
their yearning unyeilding. These geometries
are love's tired proofs: the badinage of wheel
and road and walk and lawn and drive and curb
and sign and line all flush, flushed with a soft
raillery of values laying the grids
we make with one another, a couple
talking in bed, a water glass near
the Bible, a child's torn bear in his arm.